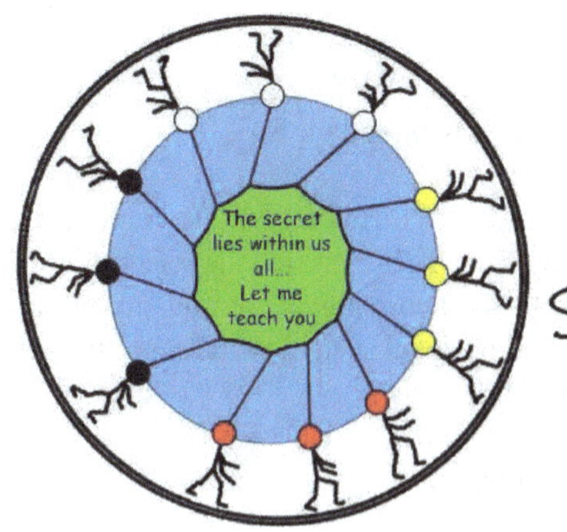

10
SECRET
STEPS
TO THE
NATIVE AMERICAN
CONNECTION
TO THE
NATURAL WORLD

By Native American Author
Dawn Moneyhan, S.C.

Moneyhan Books—Juneau, WI
ISBN: 979-8-3302-4660-1
10 Secret Steps to the Native American Connection to the Natural World
Author: Dawn Moneyhan, S.C.
Digital distribution | 2024
Paperback | 2024

Dedication

There are many who played an important role in the writing of this book. I'd like to give special thanks to Rob, John, Kathy, Shannon, Rachel, Neeyati, Jessica, Irena, Cathy, and Marcus. Without your inspiration and guidance this book wouldn't have seen print.

My heart's dedication here is to a promise I made many decades ago to my maternal grandfather, Raymond Frederick Wendorf, and a very special Creative Writing teacher at South Milwaukee High School back in 1987 - both of whom I promised to not waste my writing talent, but to instead do something important with it, make it and everything they taught me, truly mean something.

And while dedications are usually made to people, I can't omit the most important inspiration of all… my beloved and sacred prayer tree, planted in front of my house when it was built, by Harry Nelson and his family. The forced removal of this tree has lit a fire in me that I never realized existed and can never be extinguished. I couldn't save her but I can and must effect change. My fire is her last great accomplishment before her sad and tragic demise. Rest with peace my beautiful and powerful relative…now your light will never be extinguished.

Photo Credit: Dawn Moneyhan and Anonymous Juneau, WI resident donor

Preface

It's not a secret that Native American people have a different relationship with our planet. It is this very connection that sealed our fate during colonization. Our ability to remain self-efficient and self-reliant in the face of genocide, and survive - continues to perplex the world. Our steadfast refusal to abandon or sacrifice what is left of our many environmental and spiritually based cultures keeps us a threat and battling the worst of society even today. It also creates a space for those who are curious and feel an unexplained connection to our indigenous cultures and people.

Native American cultures, in their original and traditional forms, pose a threat to capitalism. Our vastly diverse cultures share a few basic structures in common, beginning with a life of planetary stewardship & environmentalism, self-sufficiency, and a tribal structure that requires care for one another as a whole people. As our many different Native American tribes begin doing the work of restoring our ancestral cultures, traditions, ceremonies, and belief systems, the threat that we will teach it to others outside of our Native American communities still looms in front of the government, Christian churches, and corporate America.

How do you control a large demographic of people? Make them needy - destroy their most basic means of survival and force them to become reliant upon that which is provided for them. This is how our Native

American tribes were conquered and continue to be controlled by the US government and Christian religions.

Basic needs such as food and shelter were the first to be destroyed. The great bison slaughter and creation of the reservation system, forced removal to lands unknown with completely different and foreign environments, were the first major impacts to our Native American tribes. This began the birth of forced capitalism in North America.

Our many tribes across North America, our great Turtle Island, are slowly but steadily reassembling the broken pieces of our ancestral ways and I am here to open the windows to the rest of the world. When enough of us "regular people" begin to put these life skills back into practice, to become more environmentally aware, friendly, and self-sufficient in our own daily lives, the impact to capitalism will be hard felt by those at the top of the economic food chain. True power will once again be returned to the people of this land.

As we begin 2024 the world is beginning to recognize that the secrets to the survival of our planet are buried deep within the shrouds of secrecy of our indigenous cultures. Though still wondering what those secrets are, the public holds back on asking us about them or listening when we attempt to share.

Since the Mayflower found the eastern shores of North America it has been asked how our Native American people can be content, or even happy, with living our cultures when we have the European way of life as an alternative?

Anyone who already knows anything true about our

ways of life, already understands. Those who come sincerely and with the intent to learn to do something different, live life in a different way, from a different perspective and approach, tend to adopt our indigenous ways for their own after experiencing them first hand. In turn they find a much more peaceful, healthy (mental and physical health) way of existing. It all begins with our connection to our beautiful planet.

I am here to guide you along this journey of reconnection - first with our Mother Earth, and then with each other - our fellow humans - the Odaawa (oh-DOW-ah) way, The KICC way[1].

On this journey we are going to take a stroll together through nature, meet the relatives you may be unaware are relatives. You will learn to listen, which will teach you to see. You will learn to reconnect with your inner spirit, an invisible bond of energy shared with every organic being on our planet, which will teach you to understand and to feel in a new way, using all of your senses.

In opening yourself to reconnecting to our natural world you will learn to channel your energy, use it to battle your weaknesses and celebrate and increase your strengths. If you follow the exercises laid out before you in these pages, in the order given, you will learn to see the world in a new light, through indigenous eyes. You will learn to uplift your own life by creating your own light, during your darkest of hours.

Where there is light, darkness cannot exist. When you possess the ability to generate your own light, darkness can never invade. The brighter your light the further darkness is always kept away. This is very

---

[1] https://www.thekicc.org/doctrine

possible. I live it every day and I am about to teach you the Native American secrets to achieve this new ability, to generate your own light. Nobody needs to be lost in darkness. Nobody needs that kind of suffering when the answers are all right under our own feet and within everyone's reach. Come—let's begin this journey of reconnection.

This isn't just a self-help book for you to read and go on about your life. This is a self-help manual, with exercises to work through in your real life, not just within the confines of this book. I am leaving plenty of space for your field notes. (If you are reading this book as a library book please commit a notebook to your journey and keep a detailed journal to keep you connected.)

My goal is to help you to create the hands-on experiences I can't bring to you in person, so you can burn them to your brain and muscle memory. This is how we humans learn most effectively. Anyone can read a book but not everyone retains that information long term. When we partake in an experience, especially one that is notable and fun, we remember.

This is the beginning of a new way of life. When you complete this manual you will have traveled many journeys in a short period of time. I encourage you to repeat those journeys and grow them forward as you learn to meet and get to know relatives you didn't know before. Let this become a family reunion as you invite the natural world into your inner circle and explore all our Great Mother Earth has to offer.

To begin you must first clear your mind of the cluttered thoughts from your day. Find a quiet place to sit alone as you read. Take time to ponder the questions asked and to work through each exercise as it is offered.

Cleansing Breaths

Take 7 deep cleansing breaths with a short pause between them. Inhale through your nose to the count of 4, exhale from your mouth to the count of 4. Let go of all you think you know about the world around you. Focus on your breathing, 1 - 2 - 3 - 4 in, 1 - 2 - 3 - 4 out. Hear your heart beating in your ears. Connect your spiritual self to your physical self.

Your body is made up of energy. Each organ functions like a well running machine fueled by this energy. It is both a spiritual energy, one of thought and instinct, and a physical energy, fueled also by nutrition. As you take in that 7th and final cleansing breath, let the physical and spiritual energy merge, becoming one energy source.

We will come back to this exercise of cleansing breaths often through this book. Practice these as a way to relax and find focus in your daily life.

We all find moments of stress and difficulties in our lives. Often these moments arise when we can't drop what we're doing to seek relaxation and peaceful thoughts. Cleansing breaths are especially helpful during these moments. We can pause anywhere we may be, without the need for extra tools or supplies, close our eyes, and focus for just a minute or two on our breathing.

Stress & tension can cause physical pain, illness, and even memory loss. As we find our focus, our muscles begin to relax, tension melts away, and our physical being improves quickly. When we improve our physical state it is reflected in our basic abilities and our mental & emotional wellbeing. We become more efficient as our bodies devote less focus on healing the physical distress and more on emotional and mental freedom.

The Science

Without the need for an intense chemistry or biology lesson, we will now work from a few basic scientific principles. This knowledge comes from Native American elders long before there were scientific papers to consult.

DNA -
"Definitions from Oxford Languages
DNA /ˌdēˌenˈā/ *Noun:* Biochemistry; noun: **DNA**

- a self-replicating material that **is present in nearly all living organisms** as the main constituent of chromosomes. It **is the carrier of genetic information**.
- the fundamental and distinctive characteristics or qualities of someone or something, especially when regarded as unchangeable."

Matter is any substance that has mass and takes up space. All matter is composed of atoms. All DNA has matter. Humans share our DNA with most things organic. We share 50% of our DNA with trees[2] and 60% with bananas[3]. We share 75% of our DNA with

---

[2] https://goodnewsplanet.com/how-much-dna-do-humans-share-with-other-animals-and-plants/
[3] https://science.howstuffworks.com/life/genetic/people-bananas-share-dna.htm

fruit flies[4] and 98% with chimpanzees[5].

Human fraternal twins share the same 50% of shared DNA[6] as humans share with trees. Everything organic is connected. When we are connected to our DNA sharing relatives the bond and communication is like that of human fraternal twins. As we strengthen and nurture this bond we learn to share even physical feelings with our relatives around us. If you've ever asked the age-old question if plants or trees can feel pain - get connected. You will learn this for yourself through your bond and relationship with those newfound relatives.

Our Native American peoples have always known this. It is in our origin stories and our legends back to the beginning of time. It is found in our ceremonies and traditions, and even within our languages. If you have ever heard our Native American peoples call others "relatives" or speak of "all my relatives" - this is our awareness and acknowledgement of the genetic connection we share with our organic relatives all over planet Earth. Our many Native American cultures are founded and built on this connection, as we nurture each bond and relationship our connection offers us. Our cultures are those of stewardship. We have a deep and instinctual understanding that if we take care of our Mother Earth she provides all we need to live and be happy, so she takes care of us.

Our cultures are often misunderstood or intentionally

---

[4] https://www.cam.ac.uk/research/features/how-close-are-you-to-a-fruit-fly
[5] Smithsonian National Museum of Natural History https://humanorigins.si.edu/evidence/genetics
[6] https://www.ncbi.nlm.nih.gov/pmc/articles/PMC6875762/

skewed to meet a personal or political agenda. There is a widespread misbelief that because our Native American peoples have always tried to explain that nobody owns the land, our great mother and provider, that it was free for the taking, as this meant we renounced or ceded ownership of Turtle Island aka North America. This has become American history's first red flag about lack of communication and misunderstanding between cultures and remains as untrue and misunderstood today as it was when the first colonists arrived.

Our planet supports and sustains all things organic, so she is respectfully regarded as our Great Mother, or Mother Earth. Her habits in nature are predominantly those of nurturing, respect, love, loyalty, and community. We learn these things from her and all our relatives, who also learn from her. We often refer to these things as wild instincts.

Our connection to Mother Earth and our recognition that we are her, she is us - there is no right to ownership there - gives our Native American peoples a different perspective of why we live, how to live properly and respectfully, and what happens while we are here in this life and world, and if we make poor choices.

For the purpose of this lesson and remainder of this book we are going to focus heavily on our connection to trees and water, 2 things we cannot exist without.

Spirituality

With the world's obsession with all things paranormal, it is well documented in 2024 that "something" exists other than us, in our world. The common and accepted definition of offered "*proof*" is "**energy**." We cannot say what specifically we experience other than the presence of another/outside/unexplained energy source that is measurable with modern technology.

It has also been immensely studied and believed by most that humans possess a soul, and regardless of belief system, religious denomination, or lack thereof, a soul is often referenced as a "spirit." Within our indigenous cultures the presence of spirits, including our own, is part of our daily life. We understand that all things organic and natural possess a spirit.

So whether we believe it to be our own spiritual power or that of the universe around us, we have just identified there is a source of energy that is not defined as "human" in the world around us.

Exercise #1

Make an ice cube. Take 1 ice cube and put it into an empty dry transparent cup/container. Set the cup in a safe place. Document how the ice melts in the cup as it warms to room temperature. Once only water remains, continue to monitor and document until the cup is empty and dry. How long does it take? Where did the water go?

- Water has the ability to transform from solid to liquid, and to gas.
- The adult human body is approximately 60% water.
- Water is matter and matter has energy.
- Water has energy.

According to the Law of Conservation of Energy - "Energy cannot be created or destroyed, but it can be transferred and transformed."

Water is the life's blood of our great Mother Earth as it is the life's blood for all organic life. We are directly connected to our Mother Earth. We already know we share 50% of our DNA with trees, now we know we share 60% of our adult bodies as water[7]. We are it, it is us. We cannot live on this planet without water. Water has matter and energy, thus water has a spirit, as we have a spirit. The energy of the water within our bodies combines with the energy within our spirit to make our bodies function, to make everything we do possible.

---

[7] https://www.usgs.gov/special-topics/water-science-school/science/water-you-water-and-human-body

Without water we can do nothing, we cannot exist.
We are connected.

Field Notes:

Electricity

According to Energy Information Administration (.gov)

"Electricity is a secondary energy source. Electricity is also referred to as an energy carrier, which means it can be converted to other forms of energy such as mechanical energy or heat. Primary energy sources are renewable or nonrenewable energy, but the electricity we use is neither renewable nor nonrenewable."

We have all felt static electricity at some time in our lives. When you pull a knit sweater over your head and your hair stands out from your head by itself - that is an experience with static electricity. When dog hair clings to your clothing and refuses to come off, sticking next to your fingers as you attempt to remove it - that is static electricity. So is that jolt when 2 people who have been fully charged, rubbing against materials that create static electricity, and then come into contact with each other.

Exercise #2

Blow up a small balloon. Tie it off with a knot, trapping the air inside. Rub the balloon on your hair 20 times and then let it go. If it sticks then your energy and the static charged energy will connect and hold the balloon in place. If you find it difficult to stick, slide your sock clad feet back and forth against carpeting or a towel for a few minutes and try again.

Rub the balloon against a bath towel, 20 times. Let it go. Does it stick? Test it against other materials. Practice manually generating static electricity and the physical bond that can be created when the energy from the static connects with the energy of the other object. Watch how pet hair, lint, and other debris in the air with an energy charge begin to collect on the balloon, and are difficult to remove.

This is an energy connection that is visible and easy to see. Our Native American cultures teach us to recognize this energy connection with all things organic. When accompanied by our Seven Grandfather Teachings[8] of honesty, truth, humility, love, wisdom, courage, and respect, this connection is present in our everyday lives. What objects/items did you find the most energy connection with as you completed this exercise? Did anything stick to you? (static electricity transference.)

---

[8] https://www.thekicc.org/doctrine

Field Notes:

Exercise #3

Hold a small organic object in your hands while closing your eyes.

Examples of small organic objects that work well - pine cones, stones, twigs, fruits & vegetables such as potatoes, carrots, etc., nuts, grass, leaves, flowers, etc.

Repeat the 7 cleansing breaths to clear the mind, and with the 7th and final breath focus your thoughts to energy. Your energy, the energy of the organic object in your hands, and repeat the words -

Matter has energy. Spirit has energy. Matter has spirit.

Continue this slow chant while focused on the DNA connection you share with the object in your hands, until you can feel a sensation, aka the energy from the organic object you are attempting to connect with.

Close your eyes and think of the water in your body, 60% of your being is flowing, able to transform from solid to liquid to gas and back again. Water has matter, has energy. Feel the energy flowing through your body and then feel the energy of the organic object you hold. Let the 2 energy sources connect, become one, as you felt with the static electricity bond. Continue to breathe slowly, deeply, while focusing all thoughts on this energy transfer between you and your chosen object - meet your relative, greet your relative. Use the power of thought energy to speak to your relative, to invite the connection. Recognize this object as matter, energy, DNA connection to yourself, a relative with energy to share and connect with your own.

Some people experience a tingling, some a mild heat generating in their hands, some describe "pins & needles" while others "a jolt like a mild static shock." It is different for each individual.

If you don't achieve this connection in your first attempt, do not give up. It is no longer instinctual for most of the human population. Don't get frustrated or feel defeated. Set down your object and try again later. Sometimes it helps to find another object. This can require practice and patience but each of us is capable of making this connection if we focus and nurture our desire to connect.
Once you are able to make the connection, test it out on everything else organic you can put your hands on safely. Take some time to meet your relatives, energy to energy, through the sense of touch.

Field Notes:

Instincts Stolen and Buried

All humans originate from an indigenous culture somewhere in the world. During our KICC Roundtable classes[9] we explored through archaeology and spirituality, the origins of the human species through evolution to the present. Face it folks, all of our ancient ancestors were cave people at one time. Our planet looked and functioned very differently than it does today.

All indigenous cultures share a number of things in common, no matter where they originated or are located on planet earth. All indigenous cultures are environmentally and spiritually based, predating all man made and currently recognized religions.

With the creation and growth of capitalism around the world, motives for living began to change. Life was no longer about enjoying the bounties of our planet as we cared for her in return, that life of stewardship. People stopped nurturing the many parts of creation that sustained our species and began to take more than they needed, to achieve a new kind of personal gain of power and man created/deemed wealth.

As capitalism continued to grow it was realized that those who continued in the old ways of indigenous cultures became a threat to the stability and continued growth of capitalistic practices. As civilized governments formed and power was claimed over fellow human

---

[9] https://www.thekicc.org/talkshow

beings, life became one of surviving a new forced way of living that brought the sacrifice of our natural world and the personal identities of our indigenous peoples across the globe.

Generations of capitalism forced the breaking of the stewardship bond between entire cultures of people all around the world. Why? Because planetary stewardship is the exact opposite of capitalism. Planetary stewardship teaches and allows us to survive by relying on our planet's natural resources without excess, without depletion, and in helping one another instead of competing with each other, against each other.

Capitalism deflates and defeats the equality we all strive for every day.

Capitalism introduced another disconnect between our human species and our planet - the lack of interaction with the natural world allowed those who were forcing capitalism and exploiting both people and the planet forward, to introduce our planetary resources to society in new ways. Today we call this "marketing."

I would be a wealthy woman today if I had a penny for every time I've heard phrases such as "It's just a tree" or "It's just an animal," etc. This learned disconnect, the removal of spirit and living qualities for all of our organic relatives, has been instilled in many generations of people so a select few can prosper.

Indigenous Cultures
A Threat to Capitalism and Patriarchy

When we understand our origins we understand how we got to this place we are today. Our current time of struggle, from climate crisis to mental health crisis, from substance abuse crisis to the crisis of violence and war around the world is suddenly vivid and defined. When we understand the true Native American history, as told by the Native American tribes & peoples throughout North America, we can trace clearly why and how our indigenous peoples posed a threat to the colonists who came from other lands, cultures, and ways of life in capitalistic societies.

All Native American cultures are self-sustaining and self-sufficient, relying only on the natural world and each other for survival and happiness, without depletion and with minimal conflict and environmental impact.

When the first colonists arrived they did so with intent. Unbeknownst to them as they journeyed across the oceans from European origins, there were hundreds of millions of thriving people, thriving civilizations already here. They came with the intent to "find riches," items of known value in their existing capitalistic societies, or new resources to which could be exploited in the same ways. Their intent was to harvest and remove these valuable resources, sending them back across the ocean to enrich themselves with materialistic goods and privileges of power.

The first conflicts between the colonists and indigenous peoples arose from the lack of comm-unication, differences in cultures, understanding, and connections to the natural world. While one newly formed society came with purpose, to destroy and deplete the land, the existing societies fought hard to stop them. It quickly became an "us or them" situation, and the genocide of our Native American peoples officially began.

What those early colonists didn't do that thousands of years of previous visitors to Turtle Island did do - they didn't take the time to communicate, learn, and understand the cultures that were already present before they set out to extinct all traces of indigenous existence. There was no thought given to respect, for the people or the land.

Through a very well thought out and planned assim-ilation until extinction program, enacted by the governments and Christian churches, the bond between Mother Earth and our Native American peoples was also gradually withered away, forcefully replaced with the newcomer's capitalistic society and the many personal agendas, prejudices, and motives that come by association.

Native American cultures offer an independence that cannot exist within a capitalistic society. How do you steal the land from people who refuse to move away from it? You find a way to control them. How do you control a large demographic of people who need and want for nothing you can offer? You force them to be needy. In forcing them to be needy you force their dependence for basic survival, and it begins with their basic shelter and food supply.

As colonization took hold in North America, the Industrial Revolution was in full swing. These 2 very different and separate societies were essentially unaware of each other, relying only on what they were told by the government and churches to know there was another society out there around them, existing at all. Separation was forced between Native American peoples and the new people, and "Indians" were said to be "heathen, evil, and savage - dangerous." They were to be feared. Everything about Native Americans and their cultures was to be feared and destroyed quickly, thoroughly. The new European society obliged.

Why this intentional and forced separation? Why the demonization & punishment of any European who met, befriended, and/or lived among the Native American peoples at that time? Well, if our indigenous peoples taught the newcomers our sustainable ways of stewardship, our connection to the natural world, then they too could live sustainable lives - unable to be controlled or forced to contribute to capitalism or a capitalistic society. If the indigenous people befriended and held too many newcomer allies in this way, capitalism and all of the riches of this new land would never be allowed to thrive, nor would those who stood to benefit from it. So the government termed our Native American tribes "the Indian problem" as it remains in the government records today.

Exercise #4

Let's make a sandwich. You choose the ingredients. Each ingredient will represent a person who "owns or produces" that ingredient and has only that single ingredient in their possession; A full container/package of whatever that ingredient is.

When the lunch bell rings each person with their single ingredient comes to the table and puts it in front of themselves. That is their lunch.

Or - each person portions it for the number of people at the table and hands it out. Now instead of 1 ingredient in front of each person, every person has a portion of each, and a full sandwich to eat. Nobody is hungry. Nobody had to source every food.

This is our Native American way of life.

The lettuce was not more or less worthy than the tomato, mayo, meat, or bread that anyone else brought. Everyone contributed what they were able, what they had to give, and everyone was equal in reaping the full meal. In today's world we call this "potluck dinner." For **Exercise #4b** - call friends and/or family together and arrange, share a pot luck meal. Each person is allowed to bring **1 ingredient** of their choice. Have fun assembling it to form a creative meal for all to share together. During the meal, discuss the benefits of this way of life and whether you can find a way to do this on a regular schedule. Once/wk, once/month, or once/yr - the important part is the effort and the lessons taken from this important time together - a time of sharing and learning about each person's contribution to the meal.

Secrecy

For over 500 years our Native American peoples across North America have been forced to live in secrecy in order to preserve our ancestral cultures, religions, traditions, ceremonies, languages, and life ways. We have suffered generations of trauma and abuse, biological warfare, and forced assimilation practices, mass reduction of our populations, and the removal of our languages and personal identities. This was all done by design and with intent for the sole purpose of breaking our connection with Mother Earth and lives of happy and healthy stewardship and independence[10].

Today I am here opening the windows on this secrecy. It is time to pull back the curtains and to let out the light we continue to understand how to generate within and for ourselves, and to share with each other. Our connection with Mother Earth is the reason we are still here and in a position to reclaim what has been lost and stolen from us all these hundreds of years later. The time has come we must share this with all of you if we are to save anyone or anything. We are not enough in population anymore to do this alone. We must all do it together. We must all teach and learn from each other in this time of the 7th fire[11], time of great need and of destruction all around.

---

[10] https://www.bia.gov/sites/default/files/dup/inline-files/bsi_investigative_report_may_2022_508.pdf
[11] https://youtu.be/IfP3imIriUk

Like our indigenous cultures and peoples, the climate crisis has also been kept mostly in secret. Those who continue to deplete and destroy our planet for economic gain and power are still misleading and misinforming society today and for the same reasons. Methodology has changed, motives have not.

The powers that be don't want me to teach this to you. They don't want you to learn it, to understand it. They especially don't want you to put it to use in your own life. If enough people in our society reconnect, take back the power of our indigenous origins and beautiful planet, we can reclaim the power of our ancestors, to shape the world around us in a healthy way for us and our planet both.

Communication

Now that you have successfully renewed this conn- ection what should you do with it? Well, the next thing that makes sense is communication.

When we meet other humans and don't speak the same language or share the same culture, what do we do? How do we function? How do we understand who does and does not pose a threat? The simple answer - we learn to listen & observe and then find a way to communicate.

Communication isn't just about oral language. There is much truth in the term "universal language." It qualifies as "body language" in human interactions. Our posture, our focused attention, facial expressions, even our breathing pattern communicates to the world around us, information about us, in each moment.

Yet there are those times we find ourselves with

intuitions - feelings we can't explain - and we aren't sure where they come from but they are strong and we just *know things* in the moment. There are moments we communicate with just a shared look between 2 people or 2 animal species.

But how many of us realize we are communicating with each motion, each tilt of the head or lifting of the arms?

We are always communicating with someone or something in everything we do. And however we are communicating, we are using our personal energy source to do it.

Once we have learned to make an energy connection we can now combine body language and other forms of communication with that energy to engage with the natural world around us.

Exercise #5

Learning to Listen
Spend 30 minutes outdoors in a comfortable safe space. Close your eyes and listen for the first 15 minutes. What do you hear? After 15 minutes open your eyes and write down what you heard.

Divide your list into 2 categories -
   1. Man made sounds
   2. Natural sounds

Spend another 15 minutes outdoors in a comfortable safe space with eyes closed. Listen and identify the difference between the natural and man made sounds. Focus on the natural sounds. Can you identify what they are? WHO they are?

Is there wind that passes through the trees? Can you hear the difference in voices from the different trees as the same wind touches them? Which tree speaks the loudest? Which tree speaks in a whisper? Are you hearing trees or bushes? Can you identify the differences?

Repeat this exercise regularly. Make it a game and write down your answers, watch your growth as you learn to hear the voices of your relatives around you, as you know and recognize the different human voices around you as individual and distinct. Learn to hear and identify all of the voices of nature around you over time, everywhere you go. Learn to pick them out above the man made noises around you as those artificial noses fade into white noise alongside them. Listening is key to learning. Learning is key to understanding. It is a cycle; a continuous cycle, just as life is a cycle.

Field Notes:

Exercise #6

During your next interaction with the public - going to the store, the gas station, the park, school, work, greeting the mail carrier, etc.

No matter the circumstances, offer a sincere smile of greetings to every person you encounter for 1 day.
- Keep count of how many are smiling already when you shine your light in their direction.
- Did their expression change when they saw your smile?
- If they weren't smiling, did they smile back?
- If they were smiling did their smile get bigger and brighter?
- How did it make you feel with each encounter?
- By the end of the day were you forcing yourself to smile at others?
- Did anyone ask you why you were smiling at them?
- Did your smile inspire a conversation?

Watch their body language -
- Did their posture straighten just a bit?
- Did their pace increase as they were walking?
- Did they appear frightened? Confused?

What is your body language while you are smiling at them? What message are you sending with your smile?

Repeat this exercise once/month until you begin to recognize the body language of people around you.
.

Communicating in Nature

Let's take what we learned about body language and alternative methods of communication among people in *Exercise #6* and apply it in nature.

Most organic beings have some method of comm-unication. When we encounter something other than human, how do we respond? How does that other respond? Can we exercise any control over these situations?

I have noticed along my journey that these questions are not on everyone's minds all the time. Who woulda thought, huh? I live my life connected to our great Aki/land[12] and all she holds. I sometimes (often) forget that the rest of the world isn't also connected the way I am. For this reason my experiences present themselves as significant and miraculous and mind boggling to people around me. These lessons you are learning with me here are going to offer you these same experiences of your own.

Life is about perspectives and there are endless numbers of those. Think of the eye of a honeybee and the many facets it holds, the many directions it can see at once. Think of the facets on a gemstone, each one catching a different ray from the same light, at the same time, creating a sparkle that humans find fascinating without understanding the connection, the lesson each of those stones offers. Each is a perspective of the same thing in the same place and moment.

12

https://ojibwe.lib.umn.edu/search?utf8=%E2%9C%93&q=l and&commit=Search&type=english

Exercise #7

Gather a group of family and/or friends. The more people you gather the more effective this exercise will be, and the more fun, too! Ask everyone to sit in a large circle or as closely as one can be made comfortably. Pick a beginning person for your circle. The person immediately to the right of the beginning is the end. The game ends when each person has had a turn. Game play proceeds to the person to the left of the beginning and continues in a clockwise direction.

The first person writes down a short phrase in secret and folds the paper, setting it aside until the end of the round. This can be absolutely anything. "The sky is blue." "Where's Waldo?" "The dog peed on the floor." Limit to one sentence, long or short.

After setting the written phrase to the side, the first person whispers the phrase/sentence to the person on his/her/their left, exactly as it is written and just once. The 2nd person whispers what they heard to the 3rd person and play continues around the circle until the last person has heard the phrase/sentence.

To complete the round the last person states out loud what they heard and then the first person reads the written phrase or sentence out loud for all to hear.

Award 1 point for each correct word that makes it to the last person.

The 2nd person in the circle then becomes the first

person and the game repeats.

When I was a child we called this game "telephone."

The purpose of this exercise is to explore perspectives based on what one hears or thinks they hear in a given moment and how their previous life's experiences contribute with interpretation.

Field Notes:

Exercise #8

Find a seemingly quiet place to sit safely alone for 10 minutes. Use a blindfold or a rolled scarf or long sock as a blindfold for yourself. Sit upright in a comfortable place and position and spend 10 minutes listening to the environment around you.

- What do you hear? Try to identify each sound you hear.
- At the end of your 10 minutes remove the blindfold and write down everything you remember hearing.
- Examine the list and look around to see if you can connect the sounds with their sources. How many can you identify the sources? How many can you see what you identified?

  Repeat **Exercise #8** at least once/wk to hone your senses and increase your listening capacity.

Field Notes:

Exercise #9

Repeat **Exercise #8** with smells/odors instead of sounds.

When you have completed **Exercise #9** compare the results with **Exercise #8**. Can you connect anything from **Exercise #8** with **Exercise #9**?

Putting It All Together

You're almost there! Congratulations on coming so far in your personal journey. You have learned some valuable tools and lessons with some fun exercises that led to hands-on experiences, which created memories. This is how I teach the world - through experiences they can and will easily remember. I don't want the world to become dependent on me to teach them in their every moment. There is 1 of me and billions of you out there.

My goal throughout this book has been to teach you independent application of this most important lesson in a way that is fun, inspiring, and encourages deep thought and spiritual connection, exploration, and a deeper understanding of our incredible existence on this planet. We carry an obligation with every breath we take. It is an obligation to our planet, who makes our existence possible and an obligation to self and each other, to make our existence pleasurable, educational, and fun.

I have brought a new perspective to the surface. By doing so I have offered insight to our still secret indigenous peoples & cultures worldwide, and allowed you a pathway forward to connecting with us, through energy, thought, and action.

I must leave you for now with the last and final lesson within this Reconnection teaching.

Exercise #10 - Application

This is your "do something" moment! Let's celebrate with a final lesson.

Go out into nature, find a safe space, and go through some of these exercises again, using your newfound connection to everything organic. Apply the listening and communication exercises in the field and meet your relatives. Remember the lessons of body language and how you present yourself to your newfound relatives. Go with kindness, humility, and respect. When you listen - learn to respond in kind, gently, sincerely, and safely for all. Put your hands on a tree and close your eyes, focus with your 7 deep cleansing breaths and feel her energy, connect to it, and then when you open your eyes, connect to everything else around you. Greet your relatives with a smile and pay attention to how they respond. This - is the new world. Embrace it. Enjoy it. Teach others about it.

Field Notes:

You're probably wondering, "Is that it?" Let me tell you there is never a limit to what we learn every day. The limits we struggle with are those we have learned to set for ourselves. Learning to recognize and apply what we learn, respecting the lessons and each other, is how we grow and learn to live the life we've been given, in a respectful, responsible, and healthy way for all.

And no, this is surely not "it" for me and my time with you, either. Please be on the watch for my next book **"Reclamation - What Does That Even Mean?"** coming out soon as *Part 2* in this series of self-help manuals. There are a lot of self-help books out there but it's time to bring the help you really need in a way that actually works, has been used & tested for 10's of thousands of years, and doesn't break your bank or schedule to accomplish it.

I will continue to encourage inclusion and self-reliance as we travel this journey together. Right here and now, in this book, we are in the moment. This journey lasts a lifetime and I am honored to be traveling it with all of you.

Until next time, safe travels.

About the Author

Photo Credit: Mary Margaret Wacker

Dawn Moneyhan is an enrolled citizen of The Little River Band of Ottawa Indians. Dawn has a long resume spanning a wide variety of venues and interests. A short list of importance to her new self-help book series:

- Teacher of tribal culture & history
- Tribal knowledge keeper
- Tribal traditionalist
- Pipe Carrier
- Spiritual leader
- Environmentalist/Activist
- Social justice activist

- Public speaker
- Former Mrs Racine
- Aquatic Medicine Specialist
- Founder & leader of The Kwewag Indigenous Culture Church
- Caretaker & advocate for our natural world
- Truth Seeker/Truth Keeper

Dawn is an admitted workaholic and offers this as her excuse:

"There is much work to be done and not many are willing to do it. If I want or need something done I must be willing to do it myself."

About *The Kwewag Indigenous Culture Church*

thekicc.org

"The KICC" was born in September 2021 after the city of Juneau, WI cut down Dawn's sacred prayer tree to make way for an expensive sidewalk project that was forced on the residents in her community, by the city council, with the assistance of the city's mayor.

The mayor and 2 city councilmen stood with Dawn, her service dog, Inday, and her husband, alongside her beloved and special tree as the mayor declared, "I don't know anything about your culture so I don't care."

That night Dawn made a vow to "...shove so much of my culture down their throats they will choke on it!"

As Dawn gathered with her husband, Rob Moneyhan, tribal elder and beloved friend, Dr Delia Ross, and close friend "Dade" Amber Sikes, a nonprofit dream of educating the public about the true cultures and history of our Native American tribes & peoples slowly came together.

Through the process of seeking nonprofit status it was realized that all Native American cultures are spiritual based, so church status was the only available that was appropriate.

Along this journey the boarding school discoveries began, giving more meaning to this church status, and expanded The KICC's mission & inspiration to teach the world a new, yet very old way to live, in harmony with our planet and each other, guided by our ancestors, spiritual connection to everything, and the descendants who carry these long cherished secrets.

The KICC is available to the public and can be contacted by way of their website: http://thekicc.org or email: thekicc3@gmail.com